What
Religious Science
Teaches

*Other books by Ernest Holmes*

# What
# Religious Science
# Teaches

Ernest Holmes

Science of Mind Publishing
Los Angeles

Copyright © 2003
Science of Mind Publishing

Published by Science of Mind Publishing
3251 West Sixth Street
P.O. Box 75127
Los Angeles, California  90020

Book design: Randall Friesen

Printed in the United States of America
ISBN: 0-917849-23-X

# FOREWORD

Religious Science is something intelligent to think about, and something satisfying to believe in, as well as being something practical to use. Regardless of race, religious affiliation, education, or social status, one may find in it the ways and means to a fuller, richer life.

Religious Science presents a message of hope, help, and inspiration, for its practice and use extends into every form of human experience. Health, abundance, harmonious relationships, success, creative activity, and all the other things that make for the good life become accessible. Rather than feel like hopeless human beings tossed about by the currents of life, we learn that as divine beings we are the master of our destiny, and prove to ourselves that it is done unto us as we believe.

The universality of the philosophy of Religious Science is evidenced by the many references to the great religions of the world found in this book.

*Science of Mind Publishing*

# The Search for Truth

Religious Science is not a personal opinion, nor is it a special revelation. It is a result of the best thought of the ages. It borrows much of its light from others, but in so doing, robs no one, for Truth is universal.

The Christian Bible, perhaps the greatest book ever written, truly points a way to eternal values. But there are many other bibles, all of which taken together weave the story of spiritual Truth into a unified pattern.

All peoples have had their bibles, as all have had their religions; all have pointed a way to ultimate values, but can we say that any of them has really pointed *the way*? It is unreasonable to suppose that any one person, or people, encompasses all truth, and that they alone can reveal the way of life to others.

Taking the best from all sources, Religious Science has access to the highest enlightenment of the ages. *Religious Science reads everyman's bible and gleans the truths contained therein.* It studies all peoples' thought and draws from each that which is true. Without criticism, without judgment, but by true discrimination, that which is true and provable may be discovered and put to practical use.

What is Truth? Where may it be found? And how used? These are the questions that intelligent people ask. They find their answer in the study of Religious Science. Shorn of dogmatism, freed from superstition, and always ready for greater illumination, Religious Science offers the student of life the best that the world has so far discovered.

It has been well said that "religions are many, but Religion is one." The varying faiths of humankind are unnumbered, but the primal faith of the race is today, as of old, the One Faith; an instinctive reliance upon the Unseen, which we have learned to call God.

Religion is One. Faith is One. Truth is One. There is One Reality at the heart of all religions, whether their name be Hindu, Mohammedan, Christian, or Jewish. Each of these faiths, limited by its outlook upon life and the universe, evolved its own specific statements of faith, called creeds and beliefs, and was henceforth governed by them.

## Spiritual Experience

Spiritual experience is always a new thing. It ever seeks to express itself in a new way. The history of religion is a history of a periodic breaking away from the older body and the formulation of a new body of disciples to whom had come new light and a more satisfying experience.

While the Universal Mind contains all knowledge and is the potential of all things, only as much truth comes to us as we are able to receive. Should all the wisdom of the universe be poured over us, we should yet receive only that which we are ready to understand. We draw from the source of all knowledge that to which we inwardly listen. Scientists discover the principle of their science, artists tap the essence of beauty, saints draw Christ into their being, because all are given according to their ability to receive.

Ralph Waldo Emerson taught of the immanence of God; of the spiritual impulse underlying all life; of the divinity of the universe, including humankind; and his message gradually permeated the sodden mass of the accepted theological concepts of the day. He wrought a revolution in religious thinking, the full effects of which we are only beginning to realize in our own time.

"Yourself," he said, "a new born bard of the Holy Ghost, cast behind you all conformity, and acquaint men at first hand with Deity. Look to it first and only that tradition, custom, Authority, are not bandages over your eyes, so that you cannot see....Let me admonish you first of all to go alone, to refuse good models, even those sacred in the imagination of men; dare to love God without mediator and without veil."..."O my brothers, God exists: There is a soul at the center of Nature, and over the will of every man, so that none of us can wrong the universe....things do not happen, they are pushed from behind."

## The Immanence of God

The central principle of the teaching of Religious Science is this immanence of God. "God is an eternal and everlasting essence." All phenomena appearing in the natural world are manifestations of the spiritual world, the world of causes. "Our thought is an instrument of Divine Mind." "Christ is the reality of every man, his true inner self. Christ is the unseen principle in Man. God is in Man." The whole universe is the manifestation of a Unity which we call God.

Religious Science believes sincerely in what is known as "the silence," that is, it accepts the teachings of Jesus that "the Kingdom of God is within."

The new sayings of Jesus from Oxyrhyncus quotes the statement as follows: "The Kingdom of Heaven is within you and whoever knows himself shall find it. Strive therefore to know yourselves, and ye shall be aware that ye are the Sons of the Almighty Father, and ye shall know that ye are in the City of God, and ye are the City."

Believing that the Universal Spirit comes to fullest consciousness in us as our innermost Self, we strive to cultivate the inner life, knowing that religious certainty is the result of an impact of God upon the soul. We seek the witness of the Inner Spirit. We call this becoming Christ-conscious or God-conscious, meaning by that, attaining Soul-certainty.

## A Practical Message

In its practice and teachings, Religious Science endeavors to include the whole life. It is not a dreamy, mystical cult, but the exponent of a vigorous gospel, applicable to the everyday needs of our common life. Indeed, this is the one distinctive tenet of its teaching that accounts for its rapid growth. Men and women find in it a message that fits in with their daily needs.

The conventional idea of the future life, with its teachings of rewards and punishment, is not stressed: the gospel is the good news for the here and now. Religion, it says, if it means anything, means right living, and right living and right thinking wait upon no future, but bestow their rewards in this life—in better health, happier homes, and all that makes for a well-balanced, normal life.

The following is a brief statement of principles which Religious Science regards as true.

*The Universe is fundamentally good.*

*Man is a manifestation of Spirit, and for It to desire evil for him would be for It to desire evil for Itself.* This is unthinkable and impossible, for it would cause Spirit to be self-destructive: therefore, we may be certain that the Spirit of Life is for, and not against, man.

*All apparent evil is the result of ignorance, and will disappear to the degree that it is no longer thought about, believed in, or indulged in.* Evil is not a thing in itself. It has no separate, independent existence and no real law to support it.

*God is Love, and Love can have no desire other than to bless all alike, and to express Itself through all.*

Many who had lost faith in God have, in this

new manner of thinking, found what their souls had sought. The emphasis is insistently on God, ever present, ever available; and on our ability to make ourselves receptive to the inflow of the Divine Spirit. In essence, this was the primal message of the enlightened prophets of all the ages, and this is the message of Religious Science.

## Science and Religion

The thought of the ages has looked to the day when science and religion shall walk hand in hand through the visible to the invisible. A movement which endeavors to unify the great conclusions of human experience must be kept free from petty ideas, from personal ambitions, and from any attempt to promote one person's opinion. Science knows nothing of opinion but recognizes a government of law whose principles are universal. These laws, when complied with, respond alike to all. Religion becomes dogmatic and often superstitious when based on the lengthened shadow of any one personality. Philosophy intrigues us only to the extent that it sounds a universal note.

The ethics of Buddha, the morals of

Confucius, the beatitudes of Jesus, together with the spiritual experiences of other great minds, constitute viewpoints of life which must not be overlooked. The mystical concepts of the ancient sage of China keep faith with the sayings of Emerson, and wherever deep cries unto deep, deep answers deep.

We all seek some relationship to the Universal Mind, the Over-Soul, or the Eternal Spirit which we call God. That we are living in a spiritual universe which includes the material or physical universe has been the conclusion of most of the deepest thinkers of the ages. That this spiritual universe must be one of pure intelligence and perfect life, dominated by love, by reason, and by the power to create, is an inevitable conclusion.

Science, philosophy, intuition, and revelation all must unite in an impersonal effort if Truth is to be gained and held. Ultimately that which is true will be accepted by all. Religious Science is an educational as well as a religious movement and endeavors to coordinate the findings of science, religion, and philosophy, to find a common ground upon which true philosophic conclusions, spiritual intuitions, and mystic revelations may agree with the cold facts of science, thus producing fundamental conclusions, the denial of which is not conceivable to a rational mind.

It goes without saying that such conclusions cannot contradict each other. No system of thought can stand which denies human experiences; no religion can remain vital which separates humanity from Divinity; nor can any science which denies the spontaneous appearance of volition and will in the universe maintain its position.

## The Discovery of Religion

Old forms and old creeds are passing, but the eternal realities abide. Religion has not been destroyed; it is being discovered. God, the great innovator, is in Its world, and that means progress is by divine authority. Through all the ages, one increasing purpose runs, and that purpose can be no less than the evolution of the highest spiritual attributes of humankind. It is the only the unessential that is vanishing, that the abiding may be made more clearly manifest.

What wonder that religious faith in our day is breaking from the narrow bounds of past teaching and expanding both in breadth and depth. It is not because people believe less in God and the true essentials of spiritual life, but because they must believe more; they are literally forced by the inevitable logic of facts to build for themselves concepts of the Infinite commensurate with the greatness and glory of the world in which they live.

As Emerson so truly said, when the half gods go the great God arrives. Religious Science is reaching out to a truer concept of God, immanent in the universe as the very substance, law, and life of all that is. The difference between the older way of thinking and the new is that we have come to see that the One Supreme Cause and Source of all that is, is not a separate Being outside Its world, but is in fact the actual Spirit of Life shining through all creation as its very Life Principle, infinite in Its working and eternal in Its essence. The universe is none other than the Living God made manifest, so that Paul voiced a literal truth when he said, "In him we live, and move, and have our being." Such is the reverent conclusion of Religious Science, a faith that is winning its way in this, our new day.

The religious implications of this new viewpoint of life are revolutionary. It means that there is a moral and spiritual order in the cosmos to which humankind is intimately related. Faith in

God is not, as many would have us believe, a retreat from reality, a projecting of the personal wish into a cosmic postulate. Faith in God is a reasonable expanding of the facts of life to their wisest and inevitable vision and logical end; it is the logical complement of a world order, every fibre of which has a theological meaning. Religious faith, in fact, is rooted in the facts and realities of the natural order, inwrought into the very texture of life. Since supreme wisdom and life are in reality all that exist (which includes humanity), religious faith is but deep calling unto deep; God recognizing His own existence and presence.

## The End of Fear

The future religion will be free from fear, superstition, and doubt, and will ask no one where God may be found. For the "secret place of the most High" will be revealed in the inner sanctuary of our own heart, and the eternal God will sit enthroned in our own mind. We can know no God external to that power of perception by which we alone are conscious of anything. God must be interpreted to humanity *through* its own nature.

Who would know God, must be *as* God, for He who inhabits eternity also finds a dwelling place in His own creation. Standing before the altar of life in the temple of faith, people learn that they are an integral part of the universe and that it would not be complete without them. That native faith within, which we call intuition, is the direct impartation of Divine Wisdom through us. Who can doubt its gentle urges or misunderstand its meaning?

This inner life may be developed through meditation and prayer. Meditation is quiet, contemplative thought with a definite purpose always in mind. Prayer is a receptive mental and spiritual attitude, through which one expects to receive inspiration.

There is a Presence pervading all. There is an Intelligence running through all. There is a Power sustaining all, binding all into one perfect whole. The realization of this Presence, Intelligence, Power, and Unity constitutes the nature of the mystic Christ, the indwelling Spirit, the image of God, the Sonship of the Father.

Christ means the universal idea of Sonship; the entire creation, both visible and invisible. There is One Father of all. This One Father, conceiving within Himself, gives birth to all the Divine Ideas.

The sum total of all these ideas constitutes the mystic Christ.

Jesus was a man, a human being, who understood his own nature. He knew that as the human embodies the Divine, it manifests the Christ nature. Jesus never thought of himself as different from others; his whole teaching was that what he did others could do. His divine nature was aroused; he had plunged beneath the material surface of creation and found its spiritual cause. This cause, he called God or the Father. To this indwelling God, he constantly turned for help, daily guidance, and counsel. To Jesus, God was an indwelling Reality, the Infinite Person in every personality. It was by the power of this Spirit that Jesus lived. He clearly understood the unity of God and humanity.

Everyone is a potential Christ. From the least to the greatest, the same life runs through all, threading itself into the patterns of our individuality. Everyone is "over all, in all and through all." As Jesus the man gave way to the Divine Idea, the human took on the Christ Spirit and became the voice of God to humanity.

Conscious of his divinity, yet humble as he contemplated the infinite life around him, Jesus spoke from the height of spiritual perception, proclaiming the deathless reality of the individual life, the continuity of the individual soul, the unity of the Universal Spirit with all people.

Religious Science, following the example of Jesus, teaches that all people may aspire to divinity, since all are incarnations of God. It also teaches a direct relationship between God and humankind. The indwelling Spirit is God. It could be nothing less, since we have Spirit plus nothing, out of which all things are made. Behind each is the Infinite, within each is the Christ. There is no boundary line between the mind of humankind and the Mind which is God.

*Religious Science teaches that human personality should be, and may become, the highest manifestation of God.* There is a reservoir of life and power as we approach the center; it is loosed and flows through us to the circumference as we realize the unity of the whole and our relationship to it. God is incarnated in all people and individualized through all creation without loss to Itself.

To be an individual means to exist as an entity. As God, rightly understood, is the Infinite Person, so the Spirit is the Infinite Essence of all individuality. Within the One Supreme Mind, since It is infinite, exists the possibility of projecting limitless expressions of Itself; but since the

Infinite is infinite, each expression of Itself is unique and different from any other expression. Thus the Infinite is not divided, but multiplied.

While all people have the same origin, no two are alike except in ultimate essence—"One God and Father of us all," but numberless sonships, each sonship a unique institution in the universe of wholeness. *All people are individualized centers of God-consciousness and spiritual power, as complete as they know themselves to be, and they know themselves only as they comprehend their relationship to the whole.*

This Presence, this inner sense of a greater Reality, bears witness to Itself through our highest acts and in our deepest emotions. Who is there who has not at times felt this inner Presence? It is impossible to escape our true nature. The voice of Truth is insistent. The urge to unfold is constant. In the long run each of us will fully express our divinity, for "good will come at last alike to all."

We stand in the shadow of a mighty Presence, while love forever points the way to heaven. Mingled with the voice of humanity is the word of God, for Truth is a synonym for God, and who-ever speaks any truth speaks the word of God. Science reveals eternal principles; mathematics, immutable laws, and illumined minds reveal the Eternal Spirit. Behind all is a unity, through all is a diversity, saturating all is a divinity.

We can no more do without religion than we can do without food, shelter, or clothing. According to our belief about God will be our estimate of life here and hereafter. To believe in a God of vengeance is one thing, and to believe in a God of love and a just law of cause and effect is another.

To believe in a special dispensation of Providence robs us of our own immediate accessibility to goodness and creates the necessity of mediums, other than our own souls, through which we must gain entrance to Reality. We cannot reach beyond the vision of our own souls. We must have direct access to the Truth.

To believe in a specialized Providence is both scientific and sensible. We are always specializing some law of nature; this is the manner in which all science advances. Unless we can thus specialize the great Law of Life Itself—the Law of Mind and Spirit—we have no possibility of further advancement in the scale of being.

The unique power that Jesus expressed was a result of his conscious union with the creative Principle which is God. Jesus realized that we are living in a spiritual universe now, and like Buddha, Plato, Socrates, Swedenborg, Emerson, and

Whitman, he clearly understood and taught a law of parallels or spiritual correspondences. The parables of Jesus were mostly illustrations of the concept that the laws of nature and the laws of thought are identical. This has been one of the highest perceptions of the enlightened of all ages.

The universe in which we live is a spiritual system governed by laws of Mind. There are not two minds, there is but One Mind, which is God. The outpush of the Mind of God through the mind of man is the self-realization of Spirit seeking a new outlet for Its own expression. Ideas come from the Great Mind and operate through the human mind. The two are one. In this way the Infinite Mind is personal to each individual.

From the infinite self-knowingness of God, our power to know arises, because our mind springs from the Universal Mind. In this way the Infinite multiplies Itself through the finite.

*Religious Science teaches that God is personal, and personal in a unique sense, to everyone.* It teaches that conscious communion with the indwelling Spirit opens the avenues of intuition and provides a new starting point for the creative power of the Almighty.

No one ever lived who valued the individual life more than Jesus. He proclaimed his divinity through his humanity, and taught that all people are siblings. Everyone comes from the bosom of the unseen Father. As the divinity of Christ is awakened through the humanity of man, the divine spark which is shot from the central fires of the Universal Flame warms other souls in the glow of its own self-realization.

We can give only what we have. The only shadow that we cast is the shadow of the self. This shadow lengthens as we realize the great Presence in which we live, move, and have our being.

*Religious Science not only emphasizes this unity of God and humankind, it teaches us that in such degree as our thought becomes spiritualized, it actually manifests the Power of God.* In doing this, it literally follows the teaching of Jesus when he proclaimed that all things are possible to them who believe.

It is written that "the prayer of faith shall save the sick, and the Lord shall raise him up." It is self-evident that the prayer of faith is a positive acceptance of the good we desire. Faith is a movement within the mind. It is a certain way of thinking. It is an affirmative mental attitude. Throughout the ages the prayer of faith has been practiced by every religion, and wonderful results have been obtained. There is a law governing this possibility, else it never could have been. It is the business of

Religious Science to view these facts, estimate their cause, and in so doing, provide a definite knowledge of the law governing the facts.

*Religious Science teaches that right thinking can demonstrate success and abundance;* can offer help to those who are in physical distress, and bring peace to those who are lost in the maze of confusion, doubt, and fear.

*Religious Science teaches that the Kingdom of God is at hand;* that there is a perfection at the center of all things, and that true salvation comes only through true enlightenment, through a more conscious and a more complete union of our lives with the Invisible.

*Religious Science does not place an undue importance either on mental healing or the law of abundance. Its main emphasis is placed not on visible things but on the Invisible.* It teaches that there is an invisible law governing everyone's life. This law is a law of faith or belief; it is a law of mind and consciousness. This will make a great appeal to the practical person, for when the Law of our being is understood, it may be consciously used, thus providing every individual with a certain way to freedom, to happiness, and to success.

*Religious Science is a religion of joy; it is a religion free from fear and uncertainty; it is a religion of faith, a faith justified by results.* Everyone is instinctively religious, and everyone has an intuition within themselves which, should they follow it, would lead them inevitably to a place not only of an inner sense of certainty, but to a place of the outer condition of security.

The Divine Spirit is not limited nor does It wish to limit us. Its whole intent is to give us a more abundant life. The time has come when religion must be made practical, and when faith in the invisible must be consciously developed, free from dogma, superstition, and fear.

Religious Science today offers the world what the ages have been waiting for. It is the culmination of the hope, the aspiration, and the faith of the enlightened of all time. The Truth it teaches is old; it has run through spiritual philosophies of the ages, but it has always been more or less handicapped by the dogmas and superstitions imposed upon it by the theology of its times.

The "new age" demands that the fear and superstition surrounding religious conviction be removed, and that the Truth—plain, simple, and direct—be presented so all people may learn to live now, in the present, with the assurance that the "eternal God is thy refuge...."

# Our Declaration of Principles

**We believe** in God, the Living Spirit Almighty; one, indestructible, absolute, and self-existent Cause. This One manifests Itself in and through all creation. The manifest universe is the body of God; it is the logical and necessary outcome of the infinite self-knowingness of God.

**We believe** in the incarnation of the Spirit in everyone and that all people are incarnations of the One Spirit.

**We believe** in the eternality, the immortality, and the continuity of the individual soul, forever and ever expanding.

**We believe** that Heaven is within us and that we experience it to the degree that we become conscious of it.

**We believe** the ultimate goal of life to be a complete emancipation from all discord of every nature, and that this goal is sure to be attained by all.

**We believe** in the unity of all life, and that the highest God and the innermost God is one God.

**We believe** that God is personal to all who feel this Indwelling Presence.

**We believe** in the direct revelation of Truth through the intuitive and spiritual nature of the individual, and that any person who lives in close contact with the Indwelling God may become a revealer of Truth.

**We believe** that the Universal Spirit, which is God, operates through a Universal Mind, which is the Law of God; and that we are surrounded by this Creative Mind, which receives the direct impress of our thought and acts upon it.

**We believe** in the healing of the sick through the power of this Mind.

**We believe** in the control of conditions through the power of this Mind.

**We believe** in the eternal Goodness, the eternal Loving-kindness, and the eternal Givingness of Life to all.

**We believe** in our own soul, our own spirit, and our own destiny; for we understand that the life of all is God.

★       ★       ★       ★

The following explanation, which is an analysis of our belief, illustrates how Religious Science keeps faith with the spiritual thought of the ages.

*We believe in God, the Living Spirit Almighty...*
    God is defined as the Deity; the Supreme Being; the Divine Presence in the universe permeating everything; the Animating Principle in everything; as Love, and the Source of all inspiration and power; the Source of guidance and of divine protection.
    God has been called by a thousand different names throughout the ages. The time has now come to cast aside any points of disagreement and to realize that we are all worshiping one and the same God.
    The sacred books of all peoples declare that God is One; a unity from which nothing can be excluded and to which nothing can be added. God is omnipotent, omnipresent, and omniscient.
    God is our Heavenly Father and our Spiritual

Mother; the Breath of our life. God is the Changeless Reality in which we live, move, and have our being.

The Bible says: "I am the Lord, I change not." "Forever, O Lord, thy word is settled in heaven." "One God and Father of all, who is above all, and through all, and in you all." "Know that the Lord he is God; there is none else beside him." "I am Alpha and Omega, the beginning and the ending...which is, and which was, and which is to come, the Almighty." "In whom are hid all the treasures of wisdom and knowledge." "God is Spirit: and they that worship him must worship him in spirit and in truth." "All things were made by him; and without him was not anything made that was made." "...there is but one God, the Father, of whom are all things, and we in him." "...the Lord he is God in heaven above, and upon the earth beneath: there is none else." "For with thee is the fountain of life; in thy light shall we see light." "God is light, and in him is no darkness at all." "Thy righteousness is an everlasting righteousness, and thy law is the truth."

From the text of Taoism: "The Tao considered as unchanging, has no name." "There is no end or beginning to the Tao." "The great Tao has no name, but It effects the growth and maintenance of all things." "The Tao does not exhaust itself in what is greatest, nor is it ever absent from what is least; and therefore it is to be found complete and diffused in all things." "Thus it is that the Tao produces [all things], nourishes them…nurses them, completes them, matures them, maintains them, and overspreads them."

The Hermetic teaching defines God as a "…Power that naught can e'er surpass, a Power with which no one can make comparison of any human thing at all…" This teaching defines God as a Oneness which is the "…Source and Root of all, is in all things…." "His being is conceiving of all things….He ever makes all things, in heaven, in air, in earth, in deep, in all of cosmos [that is in the entire universe]….For there is naught in all the world that is not He." "God is united to all men as light to the sun."

From the sacred books of the East: "There is but one Brahma which is Truth's self. It is from our ignorance of that One that godheads have been conceived to be diverse." "As the sun, manifesting all parts of space, above, between, and below, shines resplendent, so overrules the all-glorious adorable God…" "The One God, who is concealed in all beings, who pervades all, who is the inner soul of all beings, the ruler of all actions, who dwells in all beings…" "God is permanent, eternal and therefore existence itself." "All is the effect of all, One Universal Essence." "The Supreme Soul hath another name, that is, Pure Knowledge."

The Zend-Avesta defines God as "Perfect Holiness, Understanding, Knowledge, The most Beneficent, The uncomparable One, The All-seeing One, The healing One, The Creator."

The Koran says that "He is the Living One. No God is there but He."

In Buddhism we find these thoughts: "…the Supreme Being, the Unsurpassed, the Perceiver of All Things, the Controller, the Lord of All, the Maker, the Fashioner…the Father of All Beings…"

In the Apocrypha we read that God is "…the Most High who knows…who nourishes all. The Creator who has planted his sweet Spirit in all…There is One God…Worship him who alone exists from age to age…."

From the Talmud: "Our God is a living God." "His power fills the universe…He formed thee; with His Spirit thou breathest."

*We believe in God, the Living Spirit Almighty; one, indestructible, absolute, and self-existent Cause.*

In Religious Science, *self-existent* is defined as

"living by virtue of its own being." An absolute and self-existent Cause, then, means that Principle, that Power, and that Presence which makes everything out of Itself, which contains and sustains everything within Itself. God is absolute and self-existent Cause. Therefore, the Divine Spirit contains within Itself infinite imagination, complete volition, and absolute power.

We are to think of God not as *some power*, but as *All Power*; not as *some presence*, but as *the Only Presence*; not merely as *a god*, but as *The God*. Spirit is the supreme and the only Causation.

Emerson said, "There is, at the surface, infinite variety of things: at the center there is simplicity of cause." "We are escorted on every hand through life by spiritual agents, and a beneficent purpose lies in wait for us." Emerson's belief was that we are all sleeping giants:

"Sleep lingers all our life time about our eyes, as night hovers all day in the boughs of the fir tree. Into every intelligence there is a door which is never closed, through which the creator passes."

*This One manifests Itself in and through all creation but is not absorbed by Its creation.*

Religious Science defines *creation* as "the giving of form to the substance of Mind.... The whole action of Spirit must be within Itself upon Itself." Creation is the play of Life upon Itself; the action of a limitless Imagination upon an infinite Law.

What God thinks, It energizes. The universe is God's thought made manifest. The ideas of God take innumerable forms. The manifest universe springs from the Mind of God.

The Bible says that "the Lord by wisdom hath founded the earth: by understanding hath he established the heavens. "In the beginning God created the heaven and the earth." "By his spirit he hath garnished the heavens." "For he spake, and it was done: he commanded, and it stood fast." "…the worlds were framed by the word of God…" "The heavens declare the glory of God: and the firmament sheweth his handiwork."

The hermetic philosophy states that "with Reason, not with hands, did the World-maker make the universal World…"

From a Hindu scripture: "From the unmanifest springs the manifest." "Mind, being impelled by a desire to create, performs the work of creation by giving form to Itself."

Everything that exists is a manifestation of the Divine Mind: but the Divine Mind, being inexhaustible and limitless, is never caught in any form:

It is merely expressed by that form. The manifest universe, then, is the Body of God. As the Declaration of Principles reads: *"It is the logical and necessary outcome of the infinite self-knowingness of God."* God's self-knowingness energizes that which is known, and that which God knows takes form. The form itself has a Divine Pattern within it.

In the hermetic teaching we find this remarkable statement: "All things, accordingly, that are on earth...are not the Truth; they're copies [only] of the True. Whenever the appearance doth receive the influx from above, it turns into a copy of the Truth; without its energizing from above, it is left false. Just as the portrait also indicates the body in the picture, but in itself is not the body, in spite of the appearance of the thing that's seen. 'Tis seen as having eyes; but it sees naught, hears naught at all.

"The picture, too, has all the other things, but they are false, tricking the sight of the beholders—these thinking that they see what's true, while what they see is really false. All, then, who do not see what's false see truth. If, then, we thus do comprehend, or see, each one of these just as it really is, we really comprehend and see. But if [we comprehend, or see, things] contrary to that which is, we shall not comprehend, nor shall we know aught true."

One of the problems addressed by Religious Science is to distinguish between that which is temporal and that which is eternal. God, or Spirit, is the only Reality, the One Substance or Essence. The material universe is real as a manifestation of life, but it is an effect. This is why Jesus told us to judge not according to appearances.

The Talmud says that "unhappy is he who mistakes the branch for the tree, the shadow for the substance."

In Hebrews we find: "For Christ is not entered into the holy places made with hands, which are the figures of the true; but into heaven itself, now to appear in the presence of God for us."

And from Colossians: "Let no man therefore judge you in meat, or in drink, or in respect of an holy day, or of the new moon, or of the sabbath days: Which are a shadow of things to come; but the body is of Christ."

Back of all form there is a Divine Substance. Hid within every appearance there is an adequate cause. If we judge by the appearance alone, as though it were self-created, we are mistaking the shadow for the Substance.

In Fragments of a Faith Forgotten it says: "Gain for yourselves, ye sons of Adam, by means of these transitory things...that which is your own, and passeth not away.

We are to translate all creation into spiritual Causation. Then we shall be viewing it rightly. The created form has no being of itself; it is an effect. In Ramacharaka we read: "That which is unreal hath no shadow of Real Being, notwithstanding the illusion of appearance and false knowledge. And that which hath Real Being hath never ceased to be—*can never cease to be*— in spite of all appearances to the contrary."

There is a Divine Pattern, a spiritual proto-type, in the Mind of God which gives rise to all form. Jesus saw through the form to the Pattern, for he was quickened by the Spirit. "It is the spir-it that quickeneth: the flesh profiteth nothing…" "For [now] we know in part, and we prophesy in part. But when that which is perfect is come, then that which is in part shall be done away." "Now we see as through a glass darkly." That is, our spiritual vision is not quickened to a complete perception of the Divine Reality, the spiritual prototype back of the image.

All scriptures warn us to beware of false judg-ments; to judge not according to appearances, but to plunge beneath or through the objective form to its spiritual cause. This does not mean that the physical universe is an illusion; it does mean that it is a logical and necessary expression of the Divine Mind. If we were to think of the physical universe as the shadow of its spiritual Reality, we should be rightly interpreting it.

Religious Science translates physical form into mental and spiritual causation. It does not do this by denying the form, but through a right interpretation of it. The visible is an evidence of the invisible. The invisible is the cause, the visible is the effect.

*We believe in the incarnation of the Spirit in everyone and that all people are incarnations of the One Spirit.*

All scriptures declare that each person is the spiritual image and likeness of God. This is emphatically revealed in the inspiration of our own scripture which says: "God created man in his own image." "The spirit of God hath made me, and the breath of the Almighty hath given me life." "Hereby know we that we dwell in him, and he in us, because he hath given us of his Spirit." "Thou hast made him a little lower than the angels, and hast crowned him with glory and honour. Thou madest him to have dominion over the works of thy hands; thou hast put all things under his feet." "Be ye therefore perfect, even as your Father which is in heaven is perfect."

"Now there are diversities of gifts, but the same Spirit." "There is one body, and one Spirit…one Lord, one faith, one baptism, one God and Father of all, who is above all, and through all, and in you all." "One faith, and one baptism" means that through faith and intuition we realize that we are living in one Spirit, or, as Emerson said, "There is one Mind common to all individual men."

"Have we not all one Father? Hath not one God created us?" "To us there is but one God, the Father, of whom are all things." "Beloved, now are we the sons of God." "Ye are the sons of the living God." "And because ye are sons, God has sent forth the Spirit of his Son into your hearts." In other words, there is but one son of God, which includes the whole human family, and the Spirit of this son, which is the Spirit of Christ, is incarnated in everyone. Therefore, the Bible says that "he [humanity] is the image and glory of God."

"Know ye not that your body is the temple of the Holy Ghost which is in you…therefore glorify God in your body, and in your spirit, which are God's." "That which is born of the Spirit is spirit." We could have no more definite statement of the Divine Incarnation than this. Every person is an incarnation of God. Since God is the Universal

Spirit, the one and only Mind, Substance, Power, and Presence that exists, and since all people are individuals, it follows that each person is an individualized center of the Consciousness of the One God.

When Jesus said, "I and my Father are one," but "my Father is greater than I," he was stating a mathematical proposition. Every person is an incarnation of God, but no single incarnation of God can exhaust the Divine Nature. Everyone can use the figure "7" to infinity without ever exhausting its possibility. The more Divine Power we use, the more Divine Power is placed at our disposal, for "there is that which scattereth, and yet increaseth."

Not only is every individual an incarnation of God, and therefore a manifestation of Christ, but since each individual is unique, every person has access to God in a personal sense. The Spirit is most certainly personal to each one of us—individually and uniquely personal. We could not ask for a more complete union than this, for the union is absolute, immediate, and dynamic.

According to the revelation of the ages, humankind has a spiritual birthright which gives it dominion over all evil. But the old person must be put off; that is, transmuted into the new person, which is Christ. The real spiritual person is here now, if we could see him or her. It is ignorance of this fact which produces all evil, all limitation, all fear. It is a sense of separation from our Source which begets all our troubles. In the midst of the possibility of freedom we are bound. Thus, the hermetic philosophy states that though we are born of harmony, we have become slaves, because we are overcome by sleep. And the Bible says that we must awake from this sleep; that we must arise from the dead in order that Christ may give us life.

The Koran says: "We created man: and we know what his soul whispereth to him, and we are closer to him than his neck-vein."

In the Talmud we read: "First no atom of matter, in the whole vastness of the universe, is lost; how then can man's soul, which is the whole world in one idea be lost?"

The following quotations are drawn from various Hindu scriptures: "The ego [i.e., the True Self] is beyond all disease...free from all imagination, and all-pervading." "As from a...fire, in thousand ways, similar sparks proceed, so beloved are produced living cells of various kinds from the Indestructible." "If ye knew God as he ought to be known, ye would walk under seas, and the mountains would move at your call." (This is similar to the teaching of Jesus, when he said that if we had faith the size of a grain of mustard seed, we could say unto the mountain, "Remove hence to yonder place.") "There is that within every soul which conquers hunger, thirst, grief, delusion, old age, and death."

Perhaps one of the most remarkable sayings about the self in the scriptures of India is the following: "Let him raise the self by the Self and not let the self become depressed; for verily is the Self the friend of the self, and also the Self the self's enemy; The Self is the friend of the self of him in whom the self by the Self is vanquished; but to the unsubdued self the Self verily becometh hostile as an enemy." This, of course, refers to the deathless Self, the incarnation of God in us.

"He who knows himself has come to know his Lord..." This refers to the complete unity of the Spirit, or, as Jesus said, "I and the Father are one." "And he who thus hath learned to know himself, hath reached that Good which doth transcend abundance..."

From the text of Taoism are gathered the following inspiring thoughts: "Man has a real existence, but it has nothing to do with place; he has continuance, but it has nothing to do with beginning or end." "He whose whole mind is thus fixed emits a Heavenly light. In him who emits this heavenly light men see the [True] man."

Referring to the one whose mind is fixed on Reality, "His sleep is untroubled by dreams; his waking is followed by no sorrows. His spirit is guileless and pure; his soul is not subject to weariness." In spiritual revelation a calm contemplation of spiritual Truth is held important. The mind must be like a mirror if it is to reflect or image forth the Divine Prototype, the incarnation of God in humankind. "Men do not look unto running water as a mirror, but into still water—it is only the still water that can arrest them all, and keep them in the contemplation of their real selves."

The hermetic philosophy tells us that if we would know God we must be like It, for "like is knowable to like alone." "Make thyself to grow to the same stature as the Greatness which transcends all measure…" "Conceiving nothing is impossible unto thyself, think thyself deathless and able to know all—all arts, all sciences, the way of every life." It tells us to awake from our deep sleep, as though our spiritual eyes were dulled by too much looking on effect and too little contemplation of cause.

*We believe in the eternality, the immortality, and the con-*

*tinuity of the individual soul, forever and ever expanding.*

If each person is an incarnation of God, then our spirit is God individualized, and as such it must be eternal. Since it is impossible to exhaust the limitless nature of the Divine, our expansion must be an eternal process of unfolding from a limitless Center.

Immortality is not something we purchase. It is not a bargain we make with the Almighty. It is the gift of heaven. It is inherent in the divine nature of humankind. When the disciples of Jesus asked him what is God's relationship to the dead, he answered as we should expect one to answer who had already plunged beneath the material surface of things and discovered their spiritual cause. He said, "He is not a God of the dead, but of the living: for all live unto him."

God is Life, and that which is Life cannot produce death. What we call death is but a transition from one plane or one mode of expression into another. "In my Father's house are many mansions."

Jesus said to one who passed with him, "Today shalt thou be with me in paradise." In the philosophy of this spiritual genius, this God-saturated man, death was but a transition.

The Gita tells us, "He is not born, nor doth he

die; nor having been, ceaseth he any more to be; unborn, perpetual, eternal and ancient, he is not slain when the body is slaughtered."

From the Bible: "He asked life of thee, and thou gavest it him, even length of days for ever and ever." And this is the promise that he hath promised us, even eternal life." "To an inheritance incorruptible, and undefiled, and that fadeth not away, reserved in heaven for you."

*We believe that Heaven is within us and that we experience it to the degree that we become conscious of it.*

The Kingdom of Heaven means the kingdom of harmony, of peace, of joy, and of wholeness. It is an inward kingdom. This is why Jesus said that we should not lay up treasures on earth, but "lay up for yourselves treasures in heaven."

Heaven is not a place but an inward state of consciousness. It is an inward awareness of Divine Harmony and Truth. It is the "house not made with hands, eternal in the heavens." Ezekiel said, "The spirit took me up, and brought me into the inner court; and, behold, the glory of the Lord filled the house." The glory of God fills every person's consciousness who is aware of that glory.

Jesus likened the Kingdom of Heaven to a child: "Except ye be converted, and become as little children, ye shall not enter into the kingdom of heaven." This refers to the childlike consciousness, to a simple trust in the goodness of God.

The Spirit has placed divine intuition within everyone. This divine intuition is the gateway through which the inspiration of the Almighty enters the mind. This is why the Psalms tell us to "lift up our gates." That is, lift up the intuition and permit the Divine Light to enter.

When Jesus said that we are to be perfect even as God within us is perfect, he certainly implied that there is such a Divine Kingdom already established within each person. "When the without shall become as the within" then the Kingdom of God shall be established here and now. Jesus said that we should assume a childlike attitude toward this Kingdom. "Whosoever therefore shall humble himself as this little child, the same is greatest in the kingdom of heaven." "And when he was demanded of the Pharisees, when the kingdom of God should come, he answered them and said, The kingdom of God cometh not with observation: Neither shall they say, Lo here! or, lo there! for, behold, the kingdom of God is within you." This certainly refers to a state of inner awareness.

The kingdom to which Jesus referred is not external but within. It is not to be placed outside the self, "Neither Lo here! or, lo there!" but it is to be perceived as an everlasting dominion within. The Kingdom of Heaven is something we possess but have not been conscious of. It is not some far off divine event, "for the kingdom of heaven is at hand." It is neither in the mountain nor at Jerusalem, but within the mind.

Jesus likened the Kingdom of Heaven "…unto treasure hid in a field; the which when a man hath found, he hideth, and for joy thereof goeth and selleth all that he hath, and buyeth that field." The treasure of the inner kingdom is already hid at the center of our being, and when we discover it, great joy follows. Our whole desire is to possess this inner kingdom; to drill deep into the wellspring of our being and bring up the pure oil of Spirit; to tunnel the granite rock of our unbelief and at the center of our being, discover "the pearl of great price."

"And the disciples came, and said unto him, Why speakest thou unto them in parables? He answered and said unto them, Because it is given unto you to know the mysteries of the kingdom of heaven, but to them it is not given." On first reading, this sounds as though Jesus were with-holding his teaching from the common multitude, but such was not the case. He spoke in parables realizing that those who comprehended their meaning would understand his teaching, for he had already instructed his disciples in the mysteries of the kingdom. That is, he had directly taught them the inner meaning of life.

In Corinthians it says: "But we speak the wisdom of God in a mystery, even the hidden wisdom, which God ordained before the world unto our glory." This is a direct reference to the inseparable unity between God and man. God has ordained that forever man shall be one with His own being, that the kingdom of good shall forever be at hand. Since we are individuals, God has also ordained that our good shall make its appearance when we recognize it.

Emerson said that "Nature forevermore screens herself from the profane, but when the fruit is ripe it will fall." The inner mysteries of the Kingdom of God are hid from the vulgar, not because the Divine withholds Itself, but because only to the pure in heart, to the childlike in mind, can the Kingdom be revealed.

One of the greatest of the Greek philosophers said that this kingdom is something which everyone possesses but which few people use. Encased in materiality, filled with the din of objective confusion, we do not hear the still small voice which evermore proclaims, "Look unto me, and be ye saved, all the ends of the earth."

Again, Jesus likened the Kingdom unto "...a grain of mustard seed, which a man took, and sowed in his field..." He then goes on to say that very soon this small seed becomes a tree which puts forth branches. Here Jesus is referring to the Tree of Life, which means the unity of God with humankind. The seed is the consciousness of the little child which becomes aware of its relationship to the Divine Parentage. Out of this inner awareness grows and blossoms a concept of harmony. The Tree of Life expands and puts forth branches; its shade provides shelter.

No matter how small our concept of heaven may be to begin with, it has the possibility of eternal unfoldment. The power to live is within the self, implanted by the Divine. Ultimately, each one of us will realize our inner kingdom, which will become to us as the Tree of Life, providing food and shelter, perfection and joy.

Again Jesus said, "The kingdom of heaven is like unto leaven, which a woman took, and hid in three measures of meal, till the whole was leavened." He is referring to the action of consciousness of the Kingdom of God in the mind as yeast spreading through the whole lump of mortal thought, lifting the weight of the burdens of life into lightness. Jesus is referring to the Kingdom of God as the Bread of Life; the eternal Substance upon which the soul feeds; the everlasting Presence upon which the inner eye feasts; the house not made with hands in which the Spirit dwells forever.

"Again, the kingdom of heaven is like unto a merchant man, seeking goodly pearls: Who, when he had found one pearl of great price, went and sold all that he had, and bought it." Since the greater includes the lesser, Jesus told us that we are first to seek the Kingdom because everything is included in it. "Pearl" stands for purity and perfection. When we discover the purity and perfection at the center of our own being, we shall naturally sell the dross, the fear, and the doubt that infest our thought world, in order that we may possess this inner purity, that we may become conscious of this inner perfection.

Jesus did not wish us to feel that, in seeking this inner kingdom, we are losing anything worthwhile in the outer life, for he said that everyone who has sought the inner kingdom shall "receive manifold more in this present time, and in the world to come life everlasting." This is in line with all the other teachings of Jesus, that the reward for right living is immediate. The Kingdom is not something reserved only for future states; it is something which we experience here and now through the manifold blessings which the Spirit automatically bestows on us when we seek first things first.

In his parable likening the Kingdom of Heaven unto the wise virgins, Jesus clearly teaches that every person possesses the Oil of Spirit and that no person need borrow from another.

The Kingdom of God is not something we create, not something we purchase, but something that we must realize—it is something we become inwardly aware of. There is a perfection at the center of each person's being. Browning tells us that we must loose this imprisoned splendor, while Plato and his followers taught that "over yonder" there is a prototype of perfection. With them, "over yonder" had a meaning identical with the teaching of Jesus that the Kingdom of Heaven is within. The Greek philosophers taught that when the image—that is, the external—turns to its prototype, it is instantly made whole because it is instantly unified with its inner perfection.

Let us see what other bibles of the world have taught about this inner kingdom.

In the text of Taoism we find this: "Without going outside his door...without looking out from his window, one sees the Tao of Heaven. The farther one goes from himself the less he knows." "What is heavenly is internal; what is human is external. If you know the operation of what is heavenly...you will have your root in what is heavenly..." "Take the days away and there will be no year; without what is internal there will be nothing external." "He who knows...completion...turns in on himself and finds there an inexhaustible store."

The Gita tells us: "He who is happy within him, rejoiceth within him, is illumined within, becomes eternal." And in Fragments of a Faith Forgotten it says: "...the Kingdom of Heaven is within you; and whosoever shall know himself shall find it." "Seek for the great and the little shall be added unto you. Seek for the heavenly and the earthly shall be added unto you."

In the Upanishads we read: "As far as mind extends, so far extends heaven." "In heaven there is no fear...it is without hunger or thirst and beyond all grief."

The Pistis Sophia says: "Be ye diligent that ye may receive the mysteries of Light and enter into the height of the Kingdom of Light."

*We believe the ultimate goal of life to be a complete emancipation from all discord of every nature, and that this goal is sure to be attained by all.*

The ultimate goal of life does not mean that we shall ever arrive at a spiritual destination where everything remains static and inactive. That which to our present understanding seems an ultimate goal will, when attained, be but the starting point for a new and further evolution. We believe in an eternal upward spiral of existence. This is what Jesus meant when he said, "In my Father's house are many mansions."

The Koran tells us that God has made many heavens, one on top of another, which means that evolution is eternal. The hermetic philosophy taught an infinite variation of the manifestation of life on an ever-ascending scale. All evolution proves the transition of the lesser into the greater.

The original sources of spiritual thought from which the great religious conceptions of the ages have been drawn, have taught that evolution is an eternal manifestation of life on an ascending scale. As we ascend from a lower to a higher level, the limitations of the previous experience must drop away from us. Since the Kingdom of God or the Kingdom of Reality is already established in Spirit, our transition from one plane to another is a matter of consciousness, and since all persons are incarnations of the Divine Spirit, every soul will ultimately find complete emancipation, not through losing itself in God, but rather, through finding God in itself.

Tagore tells us that Nirvana is not absorption but immersion. Browning said that we are all Gods though in the germ. Jesus proclaimed that the Kingdom of Heaven is within, and that we shall attain this kingdom in such degree as we become consciously aware of and unified with it. This does not mean that there is any finality to evolution, for every apparent ultimate is but the beginning of a new experience.

*We believe in the unity of all life, and that the highest God and the innermost God is one God.*

The enlightened in every age have taught that back of all things there is One Unseen Cause. This teaching of Unity... "The Lord our God is one God..." is the chief cornerstone of the sacred scriptures of the East, as well as our own sacred writings. It is the mainspring of the teachings of modern spiritual philosophies, such as Unity Teachings, the New Thought Movement, the Occult Teachings, the Esoteric or Inner Teachings, our own Religious Science, and even much that is taught under the name of Psychology. Science has found nothing to contradict this unity, for it is self-evident.

There is One Life of which we are a part; One Intelligence, which we use; One Substance, which takes manifold forms. "That they all may be one; as thou, Father, art in me, and I in thee, that they also may be one in us."

In the Bible we find these passages: "Now there are diversities of gifts, but the same Spirit." "Whither shall I go from thy spirit? or whither shall I flee from thy presence? If I ascend up into heaven, thou art there: if I make my bed in hell, behold, thou art there...If I say, Surely the darkness shall cover me; even the night shall be light about me." "We all, with open face beholding as in a glass the glory of the Lord, are changed into the same image...by the Spirit of the Lord." "I shall be satisfied when I awake with thy likeness."

"Know ye not that your body is the temple of the Holy Ghost which is in you?" "That which is born of the Spirit is spirit." "The Lord our God is one God...He is God in heaven above and upon the earth beneath. There is none else." "...His word is in mine heart as a burning fire shut up in my bones." "And the Word was made flesh, and dwelt among us..." "...I will put my words in his mouth...the word is very nigh unto thee, in thy mouth, and in thy heart, that thou mayest do it."

All sacred scriptures have proclaimed the unity of life; that every man is a center of God Consciousness. This is the meaning of the mystical marriage, or the union of the soul with its Source. Jesus boldly proclaimed that he was one with the Father. This is the basis for all New Thought teaching, the spiritual union of all life.

The Qabbalah states that "every existence tends toward the higher, the first unity...the whole universe is one, complex. The lower emanates from the Higher and is Its image. The Divine is active in each."

Unity is a symbol of the soul's oneness with the Higher Nature, implying complete freedom from bondage to anything less than itself. All positive religions have taught that the supreme end of humanity is a union of the soul with God.

"The Atman, which is the substratum of the ego in man, is One." The hermetic teaching tells us that "this Oneness, being source and root of all, is in all." And the Gita explains that "when he [humankind] perceiveth the diversified existence of beings as rooted in One, and spreading forth from It, then he reacheth the eternal."

Again the Bible tells us: "Thus saith the

Lord…I am the first and I am the last…" "I am Alpha and Omega, the beginning and the ending…which was and which is to come…" "One God and Father of all, who is above all, and through all, and in you all."

From The Awakening of Faith: "In the essence [of Reality] there is neither anything which has to be included, nor anything which has to be added."

In one of the Upanishads we find this quotation: "The One God who is concealed in all beings, who is the inner soul of all beings, the ruler of all actions…" "All is the effect of all, One Universal Essence."

In Echoes From Gnosis we find: "Oh Primal Origin of my origination; Thou Primal Substance of my substance; Breath of my breath, the breath that is in me."

From the Bible: "To us there is but one God, the Father, of whom are all things, and we in him…" And from another bible, "All this universe has the Deity for its life. That Deity is Truth, who is the Universal Soul."

From the Apocrypha: "He is Lord of Heaven, sovereign of earth, the One existence." And the Upanishads tell us, "He who is the Ear of the ear, the Mind of the mind, the Speech of the speech, is verily the Life of life, the Eye of the eye."

Religious Science teaches an absolute union of man with his Source. So complete is this union that the slightest act of human consciousness manifests some degree of man's divinity. Man is not God, but he has no life separate from the Divine; he has no existence apart from his Source. He thinks God's thoughts after Him. He is divine neither by will nor through choice, but by necessity. The whole process of evolution is a continual process of awakening. It is an understanding of this indwelling union which constitutes the Spirit of Christ.

*The Science of Mind* defines Christ as "the Word of God manifest in and through man. In a liberal sense, the Christ means the Entire Manifestation of God and is, therefore, the Second Person of the Trinity. Christ is Universal Idea, and each one 'puts on the Christ' to the degree that he surrenders a limited sense of Life to the Divine Realization of wholeness and unity with Good, Spirit, God."

Christ is the Higher Self, the Divine Life proceeding from the Father. This Christ enters the world of manifestation and animates all things. Christ is in everything; we are rooted and centered in Him who is "the way, the truth, and the life."

Christ is the supreme ideal which Jesus made manifest through the power of his word. Christ is the Divine Nature of all being and the Supreme Goal of Union toward which all individual and collective evolution moves.

The realization of this union gives birth to the consciousness of Christ in the individual, and has been called "the light of the world." When Peter said to Jesus, "Thou art the Christ, the son of the living God," Jesus answered by telling Peter that no man had revealed this to him but that it was a direct revelation of the Spirit. This is in accord with our statement that:

*We believe that God is personal to all who feel this Indwelling Presence…We believe in the direct revelation of Truth through the intuitive and spiritual nature of the individual, and that any person may become a revealer of Truth who lives in close contact with the Indwelling God.*

"Know ye not that ye are the temple of God, and that the Spirit of God dwelleth in you?" "God is in his holy temple." Augustine said that the pure mind is a holy temple for God, and Emerson wrote that God builds Its temple in the heart. Seneca said that "temples are not to be built for God with stones…He is to be consecrated in the breast of each."

Every person is an incarnation of God, and since each person is an individual, everyone is a unique incarnation. We believe in the Divine Presence as Infinite Person, and personal to each. God is not *a* person, but *the* Person. This Person is an Infinite Presence filled with warmth, color, and responsiveness, immediately and intimately personal to each individual.

The Spirit is both an over-dwelling and an indwelling Presence. We are immersed in It, and It flows through us as our very life. Through intuition, each person perceives and directly reveals God. We do not have to borrow our light from another. Nothing could be more intimate than the personal relationship between the individual and that Divine Presence which is both the Center and the Source of each person's being.

Not *some* people, but *all* people, are divine. But all people have not yet recognized their divinity. Our spiritual evolution is a gradual awakening to the realization that the Spirit is center, source, and circumference of all being. It is in everything, around everything, and through everything, and It is everything.

The main body of the Christian religion is built upon three grand concepts: first, that *God is an Over-dwelling Presence*; next, that *God is also an Indwelling Presence*; and third, that *the conscious union of the Indwelling and the Over-dwelling, through the mind of humankind, gives birth to the divine child, the Christ, the Son of God.* It was this revelation which enabled Jesus to perform his wonderful works. He became so conscious of his union with God that the very words he spoke were the Words of God spoken through him.

The only way that the Power of God can be manifest through humankind is by our realization that it is the Father who dwelleth in us who doeth the works. Everyone should practice this close and intimate relationship between the individual and the Universal. Everyone should practice the Presence of God. This Presence is a reality, the one, great, and supreme reality of life. There is a "light which lighteth every man." Man is spoken of in the Bible as "the candle of the Lord," and Jesus said, "Let your light so shine before men, that they may see your good works, and glorify your Father which is in heaven."

Through spiritual intuition Jesus perceived his union with God. What suffering, what unuttered anguish, what persistence, effort, and discipline this man may have gone through to arrive at this exalted state, we know not, but we may be gratefully aware that he passed through every gamut of human suffering and emerged triumphant, supreme. Christ is the divine and universal

Emanation of the Infinite Spirit incarnated in everything, individualized in humankind and universalized in God.

Whatever God is in the universal, humankind is in the individual. This is why all spiritual leaders have told us that if we would uncover the hidden possibility within, we should not only discover the true Self, the Christ, we should also uncover the true God, the One and Only Cause, the Supreme Being, the Infinite Person.

Jesus taught a complete union of humankind with God. He proclaimed that all people are divine; that all are one with the Father; that the Kingdom of Heaven is within; that the Father has delivered all power unto the son; and that the son thinks the thoughts of God after Him, and imbibes spiritual power through realization of his union with his Source.

*We believe that the Universal Spirit, which is God, operates through a Universal Mind, which is the Law of God; and that we are surrounded by this Creative Mind, which receives the direct impress of our thought and acts upon it.*

This deals with the practical use of spiritual Power. Religious Science differentiates between Spirit, Mind, and Body, just as all the great major religious have done. Spirit is the conscious and active aspect of God, as distinguished from the passive, receptive, and form-taking aspect. Spirit imparts motion and manifests Itself through form. Thus, the ancients said that Spirit uses matter as a sheath.

Philo, often called Philo Judaeus, born about 10 B.C., one of the greatest of the Jewish philosophers of the Alexandrian school, said that the Active Principle, which is Spirit, is absolutely free and that the passive principle is set in motion by the Spirit, giving birth to form. Plotinus, considered the greatest of the Neo-Platonists, taught that Spirit, as Active Intelligence, operates upon an unformed substance, which is passive to It, and that through the power of the Word of Spirit, this substance takes form and becomes the physical world.

The spiritual teachings of antiquity all taught a trinity or threefold unity. In order that anything may exist there must be an active principle of self-assertion, acting as law upon a passive principle, which Plotinus called an indeterminate substance, whose business it is to receive the forms which the contemplation (the word or the thought) of Spirit gives to it. In Religious Science, following the example of the Christian scriptures, we have named this trinity, "The Father, Son and Holy Ghost." The Father, the supreme creative Principle; the Son (the Christ) the universal manifestation of the Father; and the supreme Law of Cause and Effect, the servant of the Spirit throughout the ages.

The Father means Absolute Being, the Unconditioned First Cause, the Source of all that is. Jesus called this Life Force "The Father." He referred to himself, and to all other people, as "The Son." "He is the image of the invisible God…" The ancient Hindus referred to The Son as Atman, the innermost spiritual self. Atman is the manifestation of Brahma as individuality. Man is an individualized center of the Consciousness of God. The Christian scripture refers to the same self when it speaks of Christ in us, for the Christ Principle has a meaning identical with Atma-Buddhi, which means divine illumination, "the Light of the world."

The Bible says that "the first man [Adam] is of the earth…the second man is the Lord from heaven." This refers first to the physical being, formed after the manner of all creation, and next to the Christ Principle animating this being. The birth of Christ, through Jesus, was the awakening of his consciousness to a realization of his union with

God—"I and my Father are one." Jesus clearly taught that all people must come to this realization if they would enter into the kingdom of harmony, into conscious union with God, and thus gain wholeness.

## The Perfect Way

"The first Adam is of the earth, earthy, and liable to death. The second is 'from heaven,' and triumphant over death. For 'sin has no more dominion over him.' He, therefore, is the product of a soul purified from defilement by matter, and released from subjection to the body. Such a soul is called virgin. And she has for spouse, not matter—for that she has renounced—but the Divine Spirit which is God. And the man born of this union is in the image of God, and is God made man; that is, he is Christ, and it is the Christ thus born in every man, who redeems him and endows him with eternal life."

And from the same source: "For, as cannot he too clearly and forcibly stated, between the man who becomes a Christ, and other men, there is no difference whatever of kind. The difference is

alone of condition and degree, and consists in difference of unfoldment of the spiritual nature pos-
sessed by all in virtue of their common derivation.
'All things,' as has repeatedly been said, 'are made
of the divine Substance. And Humanity represents
a stream which, taking its rise in the outermost
and lowest mode of differentiation of that
Substance, flows inwards and upwards to the highest, which is God. And the point at which it reach-
es the celestial, and empties itself into Deity, is
'Christ.' Any doctrine other than this—any doctrine which makes the Christ of a different and
non-human nature—is anti-Christian and subhu-
man. And, of such doctrine, the direct effect is to
cut off man altogether from access to God, and
God from access to man."

And from Basil Wilberforce, *Problems*: "In the
evolution of God's life in man there are no short
cuts, but a gradual unfolding of a principle of inte-
rior vitality. And the motto from this thought is,
'Rest in the Lord and wait patiently for Him,'
while the child-Christ nature within you 'increas-
es in wisdom and stature, and in favour with God
and man'."

J. Brierley, in his book *Studies of the Soul*, says:
"God as the Absolute can, in the nature of things,
only come into contact with man by a self limita-

tion . . In Christ, to begin with, we have a revelation of the Absolute in the limited. In Him, as the Church all along has joyfully confessed, we see God."

"The second coming of Christ is a symbol of the completion of the process of purification and development of the souls of humanity, when the lower consciousness rises to union with the higher." From *Mystical Religions*, and quoting from Luke, "And then shall they see the Son of man coming in a cloud with power and great glory. But when these things begin to come to pass, look up, and lift up your heads; because your redemption draweth nigh."

R. M. Jones goes on to say: "This refers to the consummation of the physical at the end of the cycle. Then as perfection of the soul-state approaches, the indwelling Christ appears in glory within the souls of the saints, or is raised above the condition wherefrom at first his descent was made. The 'cloud' signifies a temporary veil which obscures the splendour of the Highest. The 'lifting up of heads' refers to the aspiration of the minds, needful so that liberation from the lower nature may be effected." And quoting from Luke again, "Verily I say unto you, this generation shall not pass away, till all things be accomplished," he explains: "Christ here points out that each grade of evolution of qualities now existent, shall not be extinguished until the complete process of soul-growth on the lower planes has been carried out."

To return to our analysis of the Trinity—the Father is the Absolute, Unconditioned, First Cause; the Infinite Person; the Divine in Whom we live and move and have our being. The entire manifestation of the Infinite in any and all planes, levels, states of consciousness, or manifestations, constitutes the Son.

So far as we know from teachings handed down to us from antiquity, the Holy Ghost signifies the feminine aspect of the Divine Trinity. It represents the divine activity of the higher mental plane; the Breath of God, or the Law of Being. It is difficult for us to transpose the meaning of ancient symbols into modern language, but it seems to be the consensus among the scholars who have studied this subject that the Holy Ghost means the relationship between the Father and the Son, or the divine, creative fertility of the universal soul when impregnated by the Divine Ideas. If creation is to take place, there must be a Divine Imagination which is spontaneous and a creative medium through which It acts. This creative medium is the Law of Mind.

When individuals recognize their true union with the Infinite, they automatically become the Christ. They are born from the lower to a higher plane and awaken to a greater consciousness of their union with the Father—"I shall be satisfied when I awake in thy likeness."

In Religious Science, it is made clear that there is a universal Law of Mind which receives the impress of our thought and acts upon it. This Law is not God, but the servant of God.

The ancients called this Law the "Feminine." Realizing that there must be an active, energizing principle which is God (the Masculine), they also recognized that there must be a creative principle in nature (which they spoke of as Feminine), whose business it is to receive God's thought and bring it into creation.

This creative Law is the Law of Mind. It is what we mean when we say there is a Universal Mind through which the Universal Spirit operates. In other words, when we think of God as pure, self-knowing Spirit, as "our Father which art in heaven," as the Absolute, the Unconditioned, as Infinite Person and Limitless Being, we are thinking of Divine Intelligence. But when we think of the universe as Law, we are thinking of the Principle of Mind which receives the impress of our thought and acts upon it, always creatively, always mathematically, and without any respect to persons.

All great spiritual teachings have proclaimed such a creative Principle. It has been called by a thousand names, but careful analysis will show that every scripture has differentiated between God the Spirit and God the Law.

The ancients said that Spirit is the Power that knows Itself. They also taught the karmic law, which is the medium for all thought and action. Karma means the fruit of action.

When Jesus said, "The words that I speak unto you, they are spirit, and they are life," he was speaking from the consciousness of Christ which dominates the mental plane. His mind was such a perfect transmitter that it reflected, imaged, emanated, or automatically became an instrument through which the Divine worked.

Knowing that his word was in absolute accord with Divine Harmony, he found no difference between it and the Word of God. It was his implicit confidence in his divine inspiration, arrived at through a lifetime of contemplation and of conscious union with the Infinite, which gave him the confidence to say, "…till all these things be fulfilled. Heaven and earth shall pass away, but my words shall not pass away." Jesus was relying upon the Law of Mind to execute his word.

In Religious Science we are very careful to draw a distinction between Universal Spirit and Universal Mind. Religious Science is the tool we use, starting with the realization that the manifest universe is, as every scripture has declared, a logical result of the Thought of God, and realizing that man is a center of God Consciousness.

We know that in such degree as we inwardly realize the Truth, this Truth which we realize, operating through a universal Law of Mind, will find outward or physical manifestation in the world of form. This is what we mean when we say that the Spirit operates through a Law of Mind; that we are surrounded by this Mind, which receives the impress of our thought and acts upon it.

Let us see what different scriptures have had to say on this subject, starting with the Christian Bible. "In the beginning was the Word, and the Word was with God, and the Word was God." "Forever, O Lord, thy word is seated in heaven." "And, Thou, Lord…hast laid the foundation of the earth; and the heavens are the works of thine hands." "Our God is a living God. His power fills the universe…with his spirit thou breathest."

In referring to the Law of Mind the Bible says:

"Every idle word that men shall speak, they shall give account thereof...for by thy words thou shalt be justified, and by thy words thou shalt be condemned." "And they were astonished at his doctrine: for his word was with power. Be ye doers of the word and not hearers only..." "For there are three that bear witness in heaven, the Father, the Word, and the Holy Ghost: and these three are one."

The Bible is based on the premise that God is pure Spirit; that It creates through the power of Its word, and that the universe is a manifestation of Its imagination (Its imaging within Itself through knowing Itself to be what It is). God is Spirit. The Spirit speaks, the Law is invoked, and a manifestation necessarily takes form. This is the first principle.

The next principle is that humankind is the spiritual image and likeness of God, and is of like nature with God; that we are made of the essence of God, and are individualized centers in the Consciousness of God.

The Bible, then, having stated humankind's divine pedigree, and having carefully pointed out what happens to people through their misuse of the Law of Freedom, commonly called "the fall of man," the conclusion is devoted to humankind's redemption. The old prophets intuitively perceived this; the New Testament demonstrates it, for in the person of Jesus there arose a man who became so conscious of his union with good that all evil disappeared from his imagination.

Through trial, temptation, and suffering, through success and failure, this glorified soul in a sense fought the battle of life for all people and thus automatically became the savior of humankind. But when they mistook the man Jesus for the Christ Principle, the wisdom of Jesus caused him to withdraw himself that the Spirit of Truth might awaken in them a corresponding realization of their own union with the Divine.

The whole teaching of the Bible may be simmered down to this simple statement, presented to each one of us individually as though a Divine Hand delivered it unto our individual keeping:

You are one with the creative Spirit of the universe. There is a universal, divine Spirit which will inspire, guide, direct and companion you, but there is also a universal Law of Cause and Effect which sees to it that every act, every thought, every motive, must be accounted for. Finally, through suffering, you will finally learn to distinguish right from wrong; you will live in conscious union and in conscious communion with the Divine Spirit.

From then on, your words, thoughts, and acts will be constructive and you will come into complete salvation. God has done all It can for you because It has delivered Its entire nature into your keeping. But since this nature is truth, goodness, beauty, wisdom, love, and power, you can never enter completely into the kingdom of harmony until you consciously unify with harmony.

This is the balance between truth and justice, between love and reason, between true divine freedom and the misuse of the Law, which is not liberty but license. This is why Moses said, 'I set before you this day a blessing and a curse; a blessing, if ye obey the commandments…a curse, if ye will not obey the commandments."

The whole problem of evil, as stated by the different scriptures of the world, is not a problem of dealing with an entity of evil, but with the misuse of a dynamic power which, rightly used, alone guarantees freedom.

The Koran says that "whatsoever good betideth thee is from God and whatsoever betideth thee of evil is from thyself." And the Bible says of the Spirit, "Thou art of purer eyes than to behold evil, and canst not look on iniquity."

From the teachings of Buddha we learn: "For the cause of the karma [cause and effect] which

conducts to unhappy states of existence, is ignorance." "Therefore it is clear that ignorance can
only be removed by wisdom." The Zend-Avesta
says, "The word of falsehood smites but the word
of truth shall smite it." And from The Book of the
Dead: "It shall come to pass that the evil one shall
fall when he raiseth a snare to destroy thee…"

From the text of Taoism we learn: "Whatever
is contrary to the Tao soon ends." "He who injures
others is sure to be injured by them in return."

*We believe in the healing of the sick through the power
of this Mind.*

Spiritual mind healing has long since passed
the experimental stage, and we now know why
faith has performed miracles. We live in a universe
of pure, unadulterated Spirit, of perfect Being. We
are, as Emerson said, in the lap of an infinite
Intelligence. There is a spiritual prototype of perfection at the center of everything. There is a cosmic or divine pattern at the center of every organ
of the physical body. Our body is some part of the
Body of God; it is a manifestation of the Supreme
Spirit.

In the practice of spiritual mind healing, we
start with this simple proposition: God is perfect.
God is all there is. God includes humans. Spiritual

humans are divine beings, as complete and perfect in essence as is God. When in thought, in contemplation, in imagination, in inward feeling, we consciously return to the Source of our being, the divine pattern which already exists springs forth into newness of manifestation. When we clear the consciousness—that is, the whole mental life, both conscious and subjective—of discord, we are automatically healed.

Religious Science gives us a definite technique for doing this. It teaches us exactly how to proceed on a simple, understandable basis. It is a science because it is built upon the exact laws of Mind, for the laws of Mind are as exact as any other laws in nature. They are natural laws. From a practical viewpoint, this is done by making certain definite statements with the realization that they have power to remove any obstacle, to dissolve any false condition, and to reveal humankind's spiritual nature.

True mind healing cannot be divorced from spiritual realization, therefore the practitioners of this science must have a deep and an abiding sense of calm, of peace, and of their union with the Spirit. They must have an unshakable conviction that spiritual man is perfect, that they are one with God, and they must know that in such degree as they realize, sense, or feel this inner perfection, it will appear. The physical healing itself is a result, an effect, of this inward consciousness.

The laws of this science are so simple, direct, and usable that anyone who cares to make the effort may demonstrate them. Read carefully the entire section on mind healing in *The Science of Mind* and you will discover that there is no mystery about this. The reason that people throughout the ages have been healed through a prayer of faith, is that faith complies with the Law of Mind in producing an affirmative result. Faith is an unquestioned acceptance.

Faith also is a certain definite mental attitude. When Jesus said, "It is done unto you as you believe," he implied that there is a Law, a Force, or an intelligent Energy in the universe which acts upon the images of our belief. Faith is an affirmative way of using this Law, this Energy, this Force. Therefore, all scriptures have announced the necessity of having faith.

"Be ye transformed by the renewing of your mind." "Be renewed in the spirit of your mind." "Let this mind be in you which was also in Christ." "I will put my laws into your mind." "Hear, O earth, behold I will bring evil upon these people, even the fruits of their thoughts." "And he sent his word and healed them." "He forgetteth all thine iniquities; he healeth all thy diseases." "O Lord, my God, I cry unto thee and thou hast healed me." "Then shall thy light break forth as morning, and thine health shall speed forth speedily." "And it shall come to pass, that before they call, I will answer; and while they are yet speaking, I will hear." "I will take sickness away from the midst of thee." "The tongue of the wise is health." "Behold I will bring health; I will cure them…"

"Jesus turned him about, and when he saw her, he said, Daughter, be of good comfort; thy faith hath made thee whole. And the woman was made whole from that hour." "Then touched he their eyes, saying, According to your faith be it unto you. And their eyes were opened." "Heal the sick, cleanse the lepers, raise the dead, cast out devils: freely ye have received, freely give." "And great multitudes followed him, and he healed them all." "And the blind and the lame came to him in the temple, and he healed them."

In spiritual mind healing, thought becomes a transmitter for Divine Power, therefore, the thought must always be kept free from confusion.

It is interesting to note that, while all the great scriptures of the ages concur about the nature of God and of humankind, and the relationship between the spiritual and the physical, outside the Christian scriptures very little is mentioned about healing or the control of conditions through the use of Divine Power, although they all agree that when the mind reflects the Divine Perfection, healing and prosperity follow.

In the text of Taoism we find: "The still mind…is the mirror of heaven and earth…" "Maintain a perfect unity in every movement of your will. You will not wait for the hearing of your ears, but for the hearing of your mind. You will not wait even for the hearing of your mind, but for the hearing of the Spirit." "Purity and still-ness give the correct law to all under heaven."

And from the Koran: "The Lord of the worlds He hath created me and guideth me; He giveth me food and drink and when I am sick He healeth me." "And never Lord have I prayed to thee with ill success."

Jesus, the last of his particular line of prophets, was the first to introduce spiritual mind healing and to instruct his followers to practice it. People have been healed through all faiths, but the great healing shrines of the Christian belief have emphasized this more than most others, even though we do find many instances of healing through all the various beliefs.

More particularly since the advent of what has been called "The New Thought," which started in America and has since spread throughout the world, do we find great emphasis placed upon spiritual healing.

This has been a sincere, earnest, and effective attempt to get back to some of the first principles which Jesus taught. He sent out his disciples, telling them to heal the sick as a proof not only of their Divine Power, but also of their Divine Authority, and he said, "Lo, I am with you alway." Since it is self-evident that Jesus as a human being could not be with them always, common sense compels us to accept that when he said, "I am with you alway," he was referring to the Divine Power, the Christ Principle, which he used.

To speak of the *science* of Jesus is no misnomer, for he certainly knew what he was doing, and repeatedly stated that his words acted as spiritual law. It might be said of Jesus that he was a practical idealist. He did not believe that the Kingdom of God is some far off event; to him it was an ever-present reality; it was always at hand waiting merely to be perceived by the inner spiritual intuition, which is the voice of God operating through humankind.

"Faith without works is dead." Therefore, faith

should be justified through manifestation, and if we have faith we can scientifically prove this. For after all, science is the knowledge of universal principles and laws consciously applied for definite purposes.

There is a science of Mind and Spirit because there is a principle of Mind and Spirit. There is a possibility of using this science because we now understand how the laws of Mind and Spirit work in human affairs. The Principle of Mind operates through our thought, through our faith and conviction, and most effectively through an attitude of love, of compassion, and of sympathy constructively used. It is impossible to make the highest use of the laws of Mind without basing such use of these laws upon inward spiritual perception, upon a conscious realization of the union of humankind with God.

When the physician and the metaphysician come better to understand each other, they will more closely cooperate. It is self-evident that each is seeking to alleviate human suffering. No intelligent person would deny the need of physicians, surgeons, and hospitals. On the other hand, it is generally agreed that a large percentage of our physical troubles are mental in their origin, and that all have some relationship to mental processes. It is most important, then, that the work of the sincere metaphysician be both understood and appreciated.

It is not at all probable that the psychologist can take the place of the metaphysician, for just as the mere healing of the body without an adjustment of the mental and emotional states is insufficient, so the adjusting of mental and emotional states without introducing spiritual values will be ineffectual. Hence, there is an important place for the metaphysician, and his assistance should be sought.

Physician, metaphysician, and psychologist should cooperate. There should be no sense of mistrust or criticism among them. The metaphysician should appreciate both the psychologist and the physician.

In the early days of spiritual therapeutics, it was believed that one could not treat people mentally with success if they were being attended by a physician, nor if they were using material methods for relief. Now we know that this idea was based on superstition. We no longer give it any serious thought. Metaphysicians feel it a privilege to be called into consultation with a physician or with a psychologist. They have learned to appreciate the field of medicine and surgery.

The day is certain to come when the field of medicine will recognize, appreciate, and cooperate with the metaphysical field. Even today this practice is far more common than the average person realizes. (When metaphysicians stop making foolish statements or denying that their patient is ill, they will find a greater inclination toward recognition from the medical world.)

Today most physicians recognize the power of thought in relation to the body. All realize the dynamic energy of the emotions. Just as psychology and psychiatry are being introduced into the medical world, so the metaphysical gradually will be understood, accepted, and appreciated. Already many psychologists are affirming the necessity of introducing spiritual values into their practice. Who is going to meet this need unless it be the metaphysician?

Progress is inevitable and cooperation between all right-minded workers in the healing arts is certain. Let us do all that we can to remove superstition, intolerance, and bigotry which, after all, merely result in stupidity. We should unite in one common cause, not only to alleviate physical suffering but, insofar as possible, to remove its cause. If much of this cause lies hidden in the realm of mind, then surely those who are equipped to work in this realm are contributing their share to the meeting of a human need.

*We believe in the control of conditions through the power of this Mind.*

While all sacred writings affirm that when we are in harmony with the Infinite we are automatically prospered, the Christian scriptures lay greater stress on prosperity through spiritualizing the mind than any other of the bibles of the world. The Christian Bible, truly understood, is a book for the emancipation of humankind from the thralldom of every evil, every lack and limitation.

From the teaching of Moses, running through the thought of the major prophets and culminating in the brilliant manifestation of the Mind of the Christ through the thought of Jesus, over and over this idea is reiterated—that if we live in harmony with the Spirit everything we do shall prosper.

Religious Science teaches that through right knowledge, we may definitely and consciously demonstrate (that is, prove or show forth) practical results of spiritual thought. Countless thousands have proved this principle, and there is no longer any question about its effectiveness.

The greatest guide we have for this is found in the inspired writings of the Christian scriptures.

"Prove me now herewith, saith the Lord of hosts, if I will not open to you the windows of heaven, and pour out a blessing, that there shall not be room enough to receive it." "And he shall pray unto God and he will be favorable unto him." "For every one that asketh receiveth: and he that seeketh findeth; and to him that knocketh it shall be opened." "Ask, and it shall be given you." "And all things, whatsoever ye shall ask in prayer, believing, ye shall receive."

Whether we choose to call this *faith* or *understanding* makes no difference. It really is faith based upon understanding; it is belief elevated to the mental position of unconditioned certainty. For Jesus said that whoever could believe "…and shall not doubt in his heart, but shall believe that those things which he saith shall come to pass; he shall have whatsoever he saith. Therefore I say unto you, What things soever ye desire, when ye pray, believe that ye receive them, and ye shall have them."

Nothing could be more definite or concise than this statement. We must actually believe that there is a Power, an Intelligence, a Law, which will make this desire manifest in our experience.

There is a Law of Mind which follows the patterns of our thought. This Law works automatically. It will always respond by corresponding. Thus Jesus said that it is done unto us *as* we believe. The word *as* is important since it implies that the creative Intelligence, in working *for* us, must work *through* us at the level of our acknowledgment of It as working. This is working *in spirit and in truth*, and according to Law. And there must be law even in prayer if there is to be cosmic order.

Man's mind has been likened to the "Workshop of God," for it is here that the tools of thought consciously may fashion destiny, may carve out a new future.

We have been told to do this according to the pattern shown us on the Mount. This means that we are to formulate our ideas on the premise that there is an all-sustaining Power and an all-pervading Presence around us, and an immutable Law ever serving us when our lives are in harmony with the Divine Nature. Through an exact law, demonstration follows the word of faith. This calls for a surrender of the intellect to a spiritual conviction which dares to believe, disregarding any evidence to the contrary.

We must continue in faith until our whole mental life, both conscious and subjective, responds. If we would pray and prosper we must believe that the Spirit is both willing and able to make the gift. But since the Spirit can only give us what we take, and since the taking is a mental act, we must train the mind to believe and to accept. This is the secret of the power of prayer.

We need not have great intellectual attainment to understand these simple things. Jesus said that the Kingdom of Heaven is reached through child-like faith. Again he said, "I thank thee, O Father…because thou hast hid these things from the wise and the prudent, and hast revealed them unto babes."

Just as the teachings of Jesus announce the Divine Presence, so his works prove the presence of a Law which received the impress of his word and brought it forth into form. He asked no authority other than that which was demonstrated through his act. Since Jesus taught the most definite system of spiritual thought ever given to the world, as well as the most simple and direct, and since he was able to prove his teaching by his works, we could do no better than to follow his example. There are two ways in which we may do this. One is blind faith, and we cannot doubt its effectiveness; the other is through coming to understand what the teachings of Jesus really meant. Thus knowledge passes into a faith so complete that it is unshakable.

Jesus left very implicit instructions relative to prayer. He said, "Judge not according to appearances." That is, do not be confused by the conditions around you. This is the first great instruction of Jesus—to have such faith and confidence in the Invisible that appearances no longer disturb you.

Next we come to the preparation for prayer. Having shut out all appearances to the contrary, enter the closet. To enter the closet means to withdraw into one's own thought, to shut out all confusion and discord. Here in the silence of the soul, look to the all-creative Wisdom and Power, to the ever-present Substance. When we have entered the closet and shut the door to outward appearances, we are to make known our requests—"what things soever ye desire."

Next Jesus tells us that we are to *believe that we actually possess* the objects of our desire, disregarding all appearances to the contrary. We are to enter into this invisible inheritance acting as though it were true. Our faith in the substance of the Invisible is to take actual form. The Divine Giver Itself is to make the gift, but first we must believe that we have received it, and then we shall receive it—"…believe that ye receive them, and ye shall have them."

This is a veiled statement of the Law of Cause

and Effect operating in human affairs. When we have believed that we have, we have actually given birth to the form that is to be presented. Having made known our request with thanksgiving and received the answer with gratitude, we must rest assured that the Law will bring about the desired result.

"Thy Father which seeth in secret himself shall reward thee openly." Rest in peace knowing that it is done. This profound principle which Jesus announced (and the simple technique of its use in which he counselled his followers) exists today in all of its fullness. It is the very cornerstone upon which our philosophy is built.

Even in divine communion, we are dealing with the Law of Cause and Effect. Our prayer invokes this Divine Law and causes It to manifest in our external world at the level of our inner perception of Its working. Because this is true, prayer should always be definite, conscious, and active.

Prayer ties us to a Power that is able, ready, and willing to fulfill every legitimate desire; to bring every good thing to us; to do for us even more abundantly than we have expected. "Before they call, I will answer; and while they are yet speaking, I will hear." This shifting of the burden is important, for when we feel isolated, alone, and struggling against tremendous odds, we are not equal to the task before us. Life becomes a drudgery rather than a *jubilant beholding*. But if we know the burden is lifted and set upon the shoulders of the Law, then power and speed come to hands and feet; joy floods the imagination with anticipation.

The reflection of an image in a mirror is an exact likeness of the image which is held before the mirror. So the Law of Cause and Effect reflects back to us a likeness of the images of our thought. Thus we are told that we reflect the glory of God. But too often we reflect the fear and limitation of man rather than the glory of God.

We must find new meanings to life if we hope to create new images which, in their turn, will supply new reflections. Jesus told us to judge not according to appearances but to judge righteously. If we judge only according to what is now transpiring, our reflection of these images will merely perpetuate the old limitation, but if we judge righteously, that is, if we look to the omnipotence of Good, we shall create new images of thought which will reflect greater abundance.

Prayer, then, is a mirror reflecting the images of our thought through the Law of Good into our outward experiences. But are we reflecting the glory of God or the confusion of humans? Jesus carefully pointed out that before we can reach a position of absolute power, we must first have complied with the Law of Love. For the whole impulsion of the universe is an impulsion of Love, the manifestation of Divine Givingness.

The Apostle Paul said, "I will pray with the spirit and I will pray with the understanding also…" This is an instruction for us to combine spiritual intuition with definite mental acceptance. He is telling us that the gift of God is to be consciously used.

We are also told to pray without ceasing, to maintain a steadfast conviction, disregarding every apparent contradiction, obstruction, or appearance that would deny the good we affirm. "But let him ask in faith, nothing wavering. For he that wavereth is like a wave of the sea driven with the wind and tossed." "To the righteous good shall be repaid." "The minds of the righteous shall stand." "Behold the righteous shall be recompensed in the earth." "The righteous is delivered of all trouble." A righteous person means one who is right with the universe; one who lives in accord with the Divine Will and the Divine Nature; one who lives in harmony with good.

We have the right then to expect, and we

should expect, insofar as our inner thought is in tune with the Infinite, that everything we do shall prosper.

*We believe in the eternal Goodness, the eternal Loving-kindness, and the eternal Givingness of Life to all.*

The Spirit gives Itself to everyone; the Power of God is delivered to all. "Whosoever will may come." No matter what the mistakes of our yesterdays may have been, we may transcend both the mistake and its consequence through imbibing the Spirit of Truth, which is the Power of God.

This does not mean that we may continue living in the mistake without suffering from it. We must transcend it. That is, we must transmute hate into love, fear into faith, and a sense of separation into conscious union with good. When we have done this, the entire record of the past is blotted out and we are again free—freed with that freedom which the Almighty has ordained, and which humankind may claim as his own.

But liberty is not license, and the Law of Life cannot be fooled. It is exact and exacting. "Therefore," Jesus said, "all things whatsoever ye would that men should do unto you, do ye even so to them." "Give, and it shall be given."

This is a statement of the Law of Cause and

Effect, which is invariable and immutable, but which is also the plaything both of God and humankind, for while the Law Itself cannot be broken, any particular sequence of cause and effect in It can be transcended. The same law which brought poverty, sickness, and death, rightly used will bring peace, wholeness, prosperity, and life.

This is the great challenge of spiritual faith. The Christian philosophy bids us not to look with doleful introspection on previous errors; but coming daily to the Fountain of Life to be renewed in mind, thought, and spirit, we shall find that we also are renewed in bodily conditions and in physical affairs.

The Scripture boldly declares the triumph of the Spirit of Christ over all evil: Be ye transformed by the renewing of your mind; by the putting off of the old person and the putting on of the new person, which is Christ. "Lo, I am with you always, even unto the end of the world."

*We believe in our own soul, our own spirit, and our own destiny; for we understand that the life of all is God.*

All people are not only a center of God Consciousness; they are immortal beings, forever expanding, forever spiraling upward, forever growing in spiritual stature. Not *some* people, but *all* people are immortal, for everyone will finally overcome or transcend any misuse of the Law which they have made in their ignorance. Complete redemption at last must come alike to all.

What transformations must ensue, what changes of consciousness must take place before this is finally brought about, the finite has not yet grasped, but through the whisperings of divine intuition we know that even though we now see as through a glass darkly, we shall someday behold Reality face to face. We shall be satisfied when we consciously awake in the likeness of that Divinity which shapes our ends.

"Beloved, now are we the sons of God, and it doth not yet appear what we shall be: but we know that, when he shall appear, we shall be like him; for we shall see him as he is." We are all in the process of spiritual evolution, but there is certainty behind us, certainty before us, and certainty with us at every moment. The Eternal Light Will break through to wherever we permit It.

Potentially, everything that is to be exists now, but our spiritual vision has not yet become completely in tune with the Infinite. This is the high task set before us; this is the deathless hope implanted in our mind by the Divine.

The trials and troubles of human experience; blind groping of the finite toward the Infinite; the sickness, poverty, death, uncertainty, fear, and doubt that accompany us constitute the cross upon which we must offer, as a sacrifice to our ignorance, that which does not belong to the Kingdom of Good. But from this cross something triumphant will emerge, for as Emerson said, "The finite alone has wrought and suffered; the infinite lies stretched in smiling repose."

Shall we not, then, go forth with joy, to meet the new day, endeavoring so to embody the Spirit of Christ that the Divine in us shall rise triumphant, resurrected, to live forever in the City of God? More could not be asked than that which the Divine has already delivered; less should not be expected.

# Appendix: Quoted Sources

Professor Max Muller, one of the greatest European Orientalists and author of *The Sacred Books of the East,* has well said that "the true religion of the future will be the fulfillment of all the religions of the past....All religions, so far as I know them, had the same purpose; all were links in a chain which connects heaven and earth; and which is held, and always was held, by one and the same hand. All here on earth tends toward right and truth, and perfection; nothing here on earth can ever be quite right, quite true, quite perfect, not even Christianity—or what is called Christianity—so long as it excludes all other religions, instead of loving and embracing what is good in each."

Like many other religions of antiquity, the origin of Taoism is more or less obscure. According to some authorities, it is said to have begun around 600 B.C. (which antedates Confucius, who was born in 551 B.C.). The world generally associates Taoism with Lao-Tze, a Chinese metaphysical philosopher who was fifty-three years older than Confucius. It was this philosopher who must have gathered together these teachings. Archdeacon Hardwick tells us that the Chinese word *Tao*

"…was adopted to denominate an abstract cause, or the initial principle of life and order, to which worshippers were able to assign the attribute of immateriality, eternity, immensity, invisibility."

The Upanishads, the Vedas, the Mahabharata, the Raja Yoga philosophy, as well as the Bhagavad-Gita, are all drawn from the ancient wisdom of India.

The philosophy of Buddha, who was born in the sixth century B.C., is well enough known not to need any comment.

The Sacred Book of the Parsis is called the Zend-Avesta, which is a collection of fragments of ideas that prevailed in ancient Persia, five years before the Christian era and for several centuries afterwards.

The Book of the Dead is a series of translations of the ancient Egyptian hymns and religious texts. They were found on the walls of tombs, in coffins, and in papyri. Like many other sacred traditions, there probably were no written copies in the earlier days; they were committed to memory and handed down from generation to generation.

Some students believe that the books of Hermes Trismegistus, which means "the thrice greatest," originally derived from ancient Egyptian doctrine. Hermes was a Greek god, son of Zeus and Maia, daughter of Atlas. To Hermes was attributed the authorship of all the strictly sacred books generally called by Greek authors, hermetic. (Encyclopaedia Britannica). According to some scholars, the Egyptian Hermes "was a symbol of the Divine Mind; he was the incarnated Thought, the living Word—the primitive type of the Logos of Plato and the Word of the Christians…"

Fragments of a Faith Forgotten are taken from the Gnostics, those "who used the Gnosis as the means to set their feet upon the Way of God." Gnosticism was pre-Christian and originated in the ancient religion and philosophy of Greece, Egypt, and Jewry.

According to H. Polano, the Talmud contains "…the thoughts…of a thousand years of the national life of the Jewish people."

The Koran is the sacred book of the Mohammedans, consisting of revelations orally delivered at intervals by Mohammed and collected in writing after his death (Oxford Dictionary). The Koran is considered one of the most important of the world's sacred books.

The Apocrypha refers to a collection of ancient writings. The Greek word *Apocryphos* was originally used of books, the contents of which were kept hidden or secret because they embodied the special teaching of religious or philosophical sects; only the members of these sects were initiated into the secrets of this teaching (Encyclopaedia Britannica).

THE AWARD-WINNING *SCIENCE OF MIND* MAGAZINE delivers insightful educational, and uplifting articles, interviews with metaphysical leaders, and hard-hitting spiritual ideas each month. The magazine's *Daily Guides to Richer Living* provide you with spiritual wisdom and guidance every day of the year.

To subscribe to *Science of Mind* magazine, or to purchase other books by Ernest Holmes or about the Science of Mind philosophy, please visit www.scienceofmind.com, or call (213) 388-2181.

To learn more about
the Science of Mind philosophy
or the United Church of Religious Science,
please visit
www.scienceofmind.com,
www.religiousscience.org,
or call (213) 388-2181.

Science of Mind Publishing
3251 West Sixth Street
Los Angeles, California  90020